Stage Fright

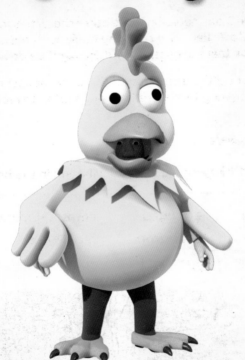

Anthony McGowan
Illustrated by Jon Stuart

OXFORD

In this story ...

Max

Cat

Tiger

Lucy

Miss Jones

Mrs Mills

X2 SPY - CAM

3

Chapter 1 – Tiger's mistake

"Now listen, everyone," said Miss Jones, to the class. "As you know, it's our turn to take the lead in the assembly this week. And we've agreed to tell the school something about the work we're doing on global warming."

"Global warming!" groaned Tiger, quietly to Max. "Global boring more like!"

Miss Jones heard him. She looked annoyed.

"Global warming is not boring, Tiger!" she said, crossly. "It's something that will affect us all. Now, who can remind me a bit about it?"

"It's about the earth heating up because of carbon dioxide," said Lucy, from the back of the class.

Assembly: Friday morning

Theme: Global warming

"Trust her!" whispered Tiger.

"That's right, Lucy," said Miss Jones, glaring at Tiger. "When people burn fossil fuels it lets a gas called carbon dioxide into the air. The carbon dioxide works like a gigantic blanket. It covers the whole earth and heats it up."

"That sounds cosy," said Tiger.

"The trouble is, Tiger," said Miss Jones, "if the planet gets too hot, ice will melt at the North and South Poles. And what might happen then?"

"Half the world might be flooded and the other half scorched," called out Lucy.

"That is bad, Miss," said Cat.

"It still sounds a bit boring for assembly!" said Tiger.

"It's a very serious problem, Tiger!" said Miss Jones crossly. "That's why I've written a play all about it for us to perform. There are parts for everyone. But, Tiger, as you find it so dull, you can have another job. You will put the chairs out before we begin and stack them away afterwards."

"Oh, Miss!" groaned Tiger.

He loved drama. Now he was sorry he'd said global warming was boring. He knew deep down that it was important.

"It's your own fault," said Cat.

"Never mind," giggled Max. "Stacking chairs might be fun."

"About as much fun as tidying my bedroom," Tiger moaned.

"Right then, the rest of you," said Miss Jones brightly. "Who wants to be a polar bear?"

Chapter 2 – Overheard

Roar!

"It's not fair," complained Tiger. "Cat, you get to be a penguin, which is probably the coolest animal in the world. Max gets to be a kangaroo … everyone loves kangaroos. But the worst thing is that Lucy is going to be a tiger. A tiger! It's terrible. If anyone plays a tiger, it should be me!" Tiger looked across the playground. "Look, she's already rehearsing!"

"Don't worry, Tiger," said Max. "I've thought of a much more important job for you."

"What?" said Tiger, brightening up.

"Well, because we're going to be in costume, we're not allowed to wear our watches. You'll have to look after them for us. We don't want anyone getting hold of them."

"Umm," said Tiger, thoughtfully. "I'll have to find a really good hiding place for them."

And he did need a good hiding place – because someone wanted to get hold of the amazing micro-watches very badly indeed ...

Chapter 3 – In a secret underground hideout ...

In a secret underground hideout, a man in a purple suit was watching a screen. His name was Dr X. Behind him were two other men, one short, one tall. They were wearing dark grey suits. They were called Plug and Socket.

"Aha!" exclaimed Dr X. "This could be the chance we've been waiting for. Finally we can get the watches back! Plug? Socket?"

"Yes, boss?" they both said together.

"Continue monitoring the situation. I have to go out."

"Are you going to your mum's for tea?" said Socket.

"That is none of your business!" yelled Dr X.

"Boss?" said Plug

"What is it? I'm late for my mu … for my appointment."

"What does *monitoring the situation* mean?"

"Just watch the screen, nitwit," Dr X replied.

"Oh, is something good on?"

"Why am I surrounded by idiots?" Dr X yelled. "Just watch the screen. Tell me if there are any developments."

"Oh, I get it," said Plug. "Sure thing, boss."

When Dr X had gone Plug turned to Socket.
"What are *developments*?" he asked.

Chapter 4 – The sunburnt penguin

The next day was the dress rehearsal.

In the play, Cat was going to be a penguin stranded on the last bit of ice left at the South Pole. Max was a kangaroo looking for something to drink because there was no water left in the whole of Australia.

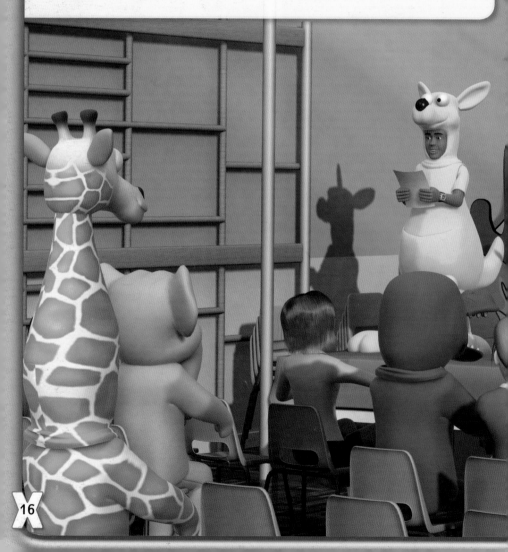

"These are some of the best lines," said Miss Jones, proudly. "Right then, let's begin from where we left off."

"What's black and white and red all over?" said Max, the kangaroo. It sounded a bit muffled.

"Nice and clear, now," said Miss Jones. "We want the audience to hear - even the ones at the back."

"A sunburnt penguin!" Cat replied, shouting out the line as loudly as she could.

"No, no, no," said Miss Jones. "It's not your turn yet. The tiger has to say *a newspaper!*"

"I don't get it," said Lucy, inside the tiger costume. "Why is it a newspaper?"

"Oh," sighed Miss Jones, "Don't you see? The ink is black, the paper is white, and it is *read* all over."

"I would be a much better tiger," said Tiger.

He had watched all the rehearsals and knew all the lines. He would have loved to have a part in the play. It was boring just putting out the chairs.

Chapter 5 – The hiding place

After the rehearsal, the children were getting ready to go home.

"Have you decided where to hide our watches yet, Tiger?"

"Yep," said Tiger, smugly.

"Where?" said Cat.

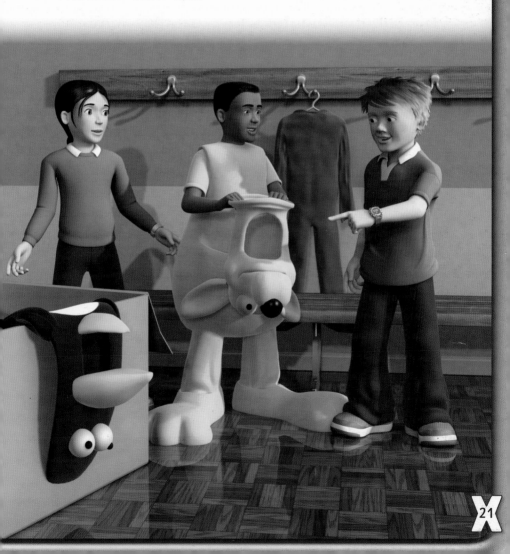

"In there," he said, pointing to a big box where all the costumes were kept.

"But everyone will be getting their costumes out. They could get lost."

"After I have put the chairs out, Miss Jones wants me to help with the costumes. That way I'll be able to keep an eye on them."

"Great idea," said Max.

The children did not know that they were being watched ...

Meanwhile ...

"Socket, wake up!"

"Eh? What? I never did it ..." said Socket, waking with a jolt. "Oh, err, anything happened yet?"

"I've been monitoring the situation. And there have been some developments."

"What sort of developments?"

"Well, they are going to hide the watches in a big box. Should we tell the boss?"

"Mmmmm ... maybe not. Let's go and get the watches ourselves. Think how pleased he'll be when we hand them over to him. We'll get a pay rise for sure."

Chapter 6 – Chicken!

It was the morning of the assembly. The children had come in early, before school started, to get things ready for the play. Miss Jones was rushing around making sure everything was just right.

"Where's Lucy?" she was saying. "Has anyone seen Lucy?"

The children had all learnt their lines. They were very excited. Except for poor Tiger. He had already put out all the chairs. He had already hidden the watches and was now helping to give out the costumes.

Suddenly Miss Jones came running over.

"Tiger!" she said frantically. "You have to help! Lucy's mum has called to say Lucy is sick!"

"Brilliant!" said Tiger. He saw Miss Jones frown. "I mean, that's awful."

"You know the lines don't you? Will you play the tiger?"

"Will I?" said Tiger.

He had already taken off his watch and was pulling his costume out of the box, before she had time to answer.

Meanwhile ...

"I said get us some disguises, you idiot," said Socket. "I didn't expect to look like a walking dinner!"

"These are disguises," said Plug. "You don't normally look like a chicken, do you?"

"I meant some dark glasses or a false beard. It's too late to change now. Just try not to stand out."

The robot spy had sent them pictures, so they knew exactly where to go.

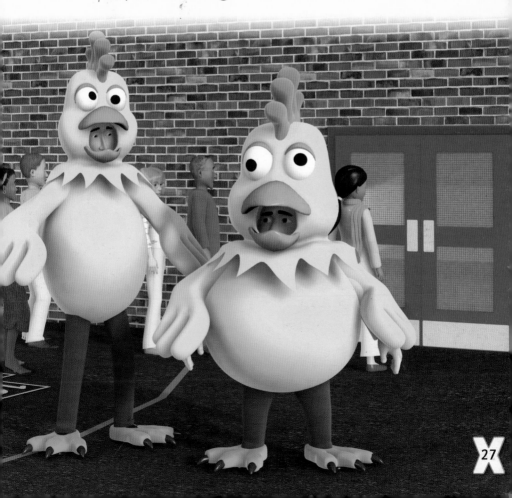

Plug and Socket flapped along to the school hall. They made their way backstage and they soon found the fancy-dress box.

"All the kids are out on stage. There's no one around. Let's get the watches and get out of here," said Socket.

"I can't find them!" said Plug.

"Keep looking," Socket replied. "We know they're in there, somewhere."

Just then they heard a noise.

"What are you two doing back here?" said Mrs Mills, the head teacher. "You should be with the others!"

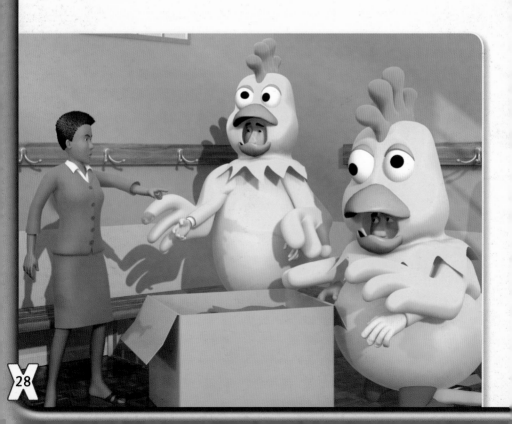

Mrs Mills pushed them towards the hall.
"Err," said Plug.
"We can't ..." said Socket.
"Not chicken are you?" joked Mrs Mills.
"Sorry," said Plug, beginning to back away.
"We've got stage flight," said Socket. "I mean, stage fright!"
They both turned and ran.

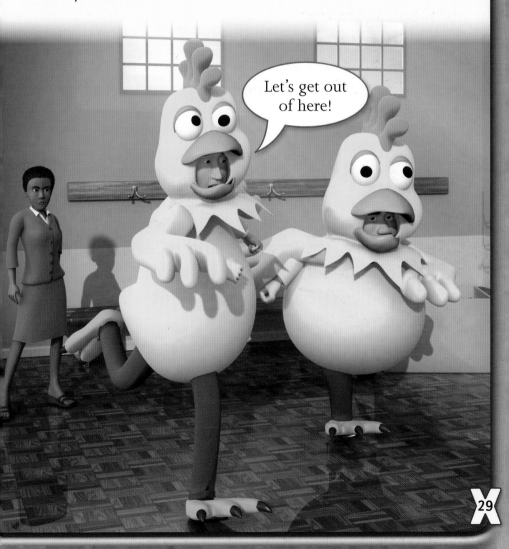

Out on stage, the play was going very well.
The children, teachers and families in the audience
were learning lots about global warming.

Cat had delivered her lines and now it was
Max's turn.

"What's black and white and red all over?"
he said clearly.

Tiger stepped forwards …

"A newspaper!" he said loudly.

"And a sunburnt penguin!" shouted Cat.

The audience burst into loud laughter and began
to applaud.

"You were great, Tiger," said Max, after the play.

"Yeah," said Cat, "and you hadn't had any rehearsals."

"I'd seen them all though," said Tiger.

"Better get our watches back now, Tiger. Where are they?"

"You had them all the time, Max."

"What?"

"They're in your pouch!"

Max put his hand into the pocket of his kangaroo costume and pulled out the three watches.

"Genius!" said Max.

Meanwhile ...

Dr X was back.

"Hello, boss," said Socket. "How was Mrs X?"

"Oh, she's fine ..." Then he growled. "Have there been any interesting developments?"

"Nothing," said Plug

"Nothing?" said Dr X. "Nothing at all?"

"No," said Socket. "In fact, er ... they cancelled the play. So the children never took off the watches at all!"

"What? Another perfectly good plan ruined!" said Dr X angrily.

Plug and Socket kept very quiet.